NELS

C000175395

The Centenary of Trafalgar

Copyright © 2013 Read Books Ltd.
This book is copyright and may not be
reproduced or copied in any way without
the express permission of the publisher in writing

British Library Cataloguing-in-Publication Data
A catalogue record for this book is available from the
British Library

Horatio Nelson

Horatio Nelson, 1st Viscount Nelson, was a British flag officer in the Royal Navy. He is famed for the part he played in the Napoleonic Wars, most notable amongst his victories being that at the Battle of Trafalgar in 1805.

Born on 29th September 1758 in Norfolk, England, Nelson was the sixth of eleven children born to the Reverend Edmund Nelson and his wife Catherine. His family were well connected; his mother being the grandniece of Robert Walpole (1676-1745), 1st Earl of Oxford, and the *de facto* first Prime Minister of Great Britain, and his godfather, after whom he was named, being 2nd Baron Walpole, of Wolterton, Horatio Walpole (1723-1809). Young Horatio attended Paston Grammar School until the age of 12 when he began his naval career. As an Ordinary Seaman and coxswain, Nelson started his naval career serving under his uncle, Captain Maurice Suckling, on the third-rate HMS Raissonable. Soon after reporting aboard he began his officer training. Unfortunately, Nelson discovered that he was vulnerable to terrible bouts of sea-sickness, a complaint that he was condemned to endure for the rest of his life.

At the age of 20 Nelson was made a captain, going on to serve in the West Indies, the Baltic, and Canada. On his return, with new bride Frances Nesbet, he found himself without command and reduced to half pay. However, following Britain's entrance to the French Revolutionary Wars, in 1793, Nelson found himself in charge of the Agamemnon. During the campaign in the Mediterranean, he lost the sight in his right eye in a battle at Calvi. Not long after, he lost his right arm at the Battle of Santa Cruz de Tenerife.

Nelson was known for being a bold and fearless commander, often to the dismay of his superiors. On one occasion he even defied orders from senior officers to cease action, putting the telescope to his blind eye and claiming he couldn't see their signals. This self-assured attitude did not prevent him from rising through the ranks however. His victories spoke for themselves. One such victory was the triumph of the Battle of the Nile (in 1798) where Nelson destroyed Napoleon's fleet and thus thwarted his ambition to establish a trade route to India.

Although still married, Nelson fell in love with another woman following his posting to Naples. Emma Hamilton, herself married, and Nelson began a lifelong love affair in which they had a daughter together, Horatia, in 1801. In the same year, Nelson was promoted to vice-admiral. He was supremely successful in his position in charge of the British fleet. The Royal Navy won many battles under his command and averted the threat of invasion from the ambitious Napoleon. It was the naval engagement of the Battle of Trafalgar (21st October 1805) that still cements Nelson's place in the history of British warfare however.

This was the most decisive battle of the campaign to stop the French and Spanish Navies, during the War of the Third Coalition (August-December 1805). Aboard the HMS Victory, Nelson led a fleet of 27 ships into battle against 33 enemy vessels just west of Cape Trafalgar, off the coast of Spain. Nelson deviated from conventional naval strategy, dividing his smaller force into two columns directed perpendicularly against the enemy fleet. The tactic worked and the battle was won. However, Nelson was mortally wounded during the engagement, shot by a French sniper.

He was shot in the left shoulder, with the bullet passing through his back.

Despite this injury, as he was being carried below by his men, Nelson asked them to pause while he gave some advice to the midshipman on the handling of the tiller, and then draped a handkerchief over his face to avoid causing alarm amongst the crew. He died on 21st October, 1805. Nelson's body was transported back to England preserved in brandy, and he was subsequently given a state funeral. The first tribute to Nelson was fittingly offered at sea by sailors of Vice-Admiral Dmitry Senyavin's passing Russian squadron, which saluted on learning of the death.

NELSON: THE CENTENARY OF TRAFALGAR.

BY ADMIRAL SIR CYPRIAN BRIDGE, G.C.B.

[The following article was read as an address, in compliance with the request of its Council, at the annual meeting of the Navy Records Society in July 1905. It was, and indeed is still, my opinion, as stated to the meeting in some prefatory remarks, that the address would have come better from a professed historian, several members of the Society being well known as entitled to that designation. The Council, however, considered that, as Nelson's tactical principles and achievements should be dealt with, it would be better for the address to be delivered by a naval officer—one, moreover, who had personal experience of the manœuvres of fleets under sail. Space would not suffice for treating of Nelson's merits as a strategist, though they are as great as those which he possessed as a tactician.]

CENTENARY commemorations are common enough; but the commemoration of Nelson has a characteristic which distinguishes it from most, if not from all, others. In these days we forget soon. What place is still kept in our memories by even the most illustrious of those who have but recently left us ? It is not only that we do not remember their wishes and injunctions; their existence has almost faded from our recollection. It is not difficult to persuade people to commemorate a departed worthy; but in most cases industry has to take the place of enthusiasm, and moribund or extinct remembrances have to be galvanized by assiduity into a semblance of life. In the case of Nelson the conditions are very different. He may have been misunderstood; even by his professional descendants his acts and doctrines may have been misinterpreted; but he has never been forgotten.

The time has now come when we can specially do honour to Nelson's memory without wounding the feelings of other nations. There is no need to exult over or even to expatiate on the defeats of others. In recalling the past it is more dignified as regards ourselves, and more considerate of the honour of our great Admiral, to think of the valour and self-devotion rather than the misfortunes of those against whom he fought. We can do full justice to Nelson's memory without reopening old wounds.

The first thing to be noted concerning him is that he is the only man who has ever lived who by universal consent is without a peer. This is said in full view of the new constellation rising above

A

the Eastern horizon; for that constellation, brilliant as it is, has not yet reached the meridian. In every walk of life, except that which Nelson chose as his own, you will find several competitors for the first place, each one of whom will have many supporters. Alexander of Macedon, Hannibal, Cæsar, Marlborough, Frederick the Great, and Napoleon have been severally put forward for the palm of generalship. To those who would acclaim Richelieu as the first of statesmen, others would oppose Chatham, or William Pitt, or Cavour, or Bismarck, or Marquis Ito. Who was the first of sculptors? who the first of painters? who the first of poets? In every case there is a great difference of opinion. Ask, however, who was the first of admirals, and the unanimous reply will still be—'Nelson,' tried as he was by many years of high command in war. It is not only amongst his fellow-countrymen that his pre-eminence is acknowledged. Foreigners admit it as readily as we proclaim it ourselves.

We may consider what it was that gave Nelson this unique position among men. The early conditions of his naval career were certainly not favourable to him. It is true that he was promoted when young; but so were many other officers. Nelson was made a commander only a few months after the outbreak of war between Great Britain and France, and was made a post-captain within a few days of the declaration of war by Spain. An officer holding a rank qualifying him for command at the outset of a great war might well have looked confidently forward to exceptional opportunities of distinguishing himself. Even in our own days, when some trifling campaign is about to be carried on, the officers who are employed where they can take no part in it vehemently lament their ill fortune. How much more disheartening must it have been to be excluded from active participation in a great and long-continued conflict! This was Nelson's case. As far as his hopes of gaining distinction were concerned, fate seemed to persecute him pertinaciously. He was a captain of more than four years' seniority when the Treaty of Versailles put an end to the war of American independence. Yet, with the exception of the brief Nicaragua expedition—which by the side of the important occurrences of grand naval campaigns must have seemed in-significant—his services during all those years of hostilities were uneventful, and even humdrum. He seemed to miss every important operation; and when the war ended—we may almost say—he had never seen a ship fire a broadside in anger.

There then came what promised to be, and in fact turned out to be, a long period of peace. With no distinguished war service to point to, and with the prospect before him of only uneventful employment, or no employment afloat at all, Nelson might well have been disheartened to the verge of despondency. That he was not disheartened, but, instead thereof, made a name for himself in such unfavourable circumstances must be accepted as one of the most convincing proofs of his rare force of character. To have attracted the notice, and to have secured the confidence, of so great a sea-officer as Lord Hood constituted a distinction which could have been won only by merit so considerable that it could not long remain unrecognised. The war of American independence had still seven months to run when Lord Hood pointed to Nelson as an officer to be consulted on 'questions relative to naval tactics.' Professor Laughton tells us that at that time Nelson had never served with a fleet. Lord Hood was one of the last men in the world to go out of his way to pay to a youthful subordinate an empty compliment, and we may confidently base our estimate of an officer's merits on Lord Hood's belief in them.

He, no doubt, gave a wide signification to the term 'tactics,' and used it as embracing all that is included in the phrase 'conduct of war.' He must have found out, from conversations with, and from the remarks of, the young captain, whom he treated as intimately as if he was his son, that the latter was already, what he continued to be till the end, viz. a student of naval warfare. This point deserves particular attention. The officers of the Navy of the present day, period of peace though it be, can imitate Nelson at least in this. He had to wait a long time before he could translate into brilliant action the result of his tactical studies. Fourteen years after Lord Hood spoke of him as above related, by a 'spontaneous and sudden act, for which he had no authority by signal or otherwise, except his own judgment and quick perceptions,' Nelson entirely defeated the movement of the enemy's fleet, contributed to the winning of a great victory, and, as Captain Mahan tells us, 'emerged from merely personal distinction to national renown.' The justification of dwelling on this is to be found in the necessity, even at this day, of preventing the repetition of mistakes concerning Nelson's qualities and disposition. His recent biographers, Captain Mahan and Professor Laughton, feel constrained to tell us over and over again that Nelson's predominant characteristic was not mere 'headlong valour and instinct for fighting'; that he was not the man 'to run needless and useless risks' in battle. 'The breadth and acuteness of Nelson's intellect,' says Mahan, 'have been too much overlooked in the admiration excited by his unusually grand moral endowments of resolution, dash, and fearlessness of responsibility!'

In forming a true conception of what Nelson was, the publications of the 'Navy Records Society' will help us greatly. There is something very remarkable in the way in which Mr. Gutteridge's volume [1] not only confirms Captain Mahan's refutation of the aspersions on Nelson's honour and humanity, but also establishes Professor Laughton's conclusions, reached ten years ago, that it was the orders given to him, and not his amour, which detained him at Naples at a well-known epoch. The last volume issued by the Society, that of Mr. Julian Corbett,[2] is, I venture to affirm, the most useful to naval officers that has yet appeared among the Society's publications. It will provide them with an admirable historical introduction to the study of tactics, and greatly help them in ascertaining the importance of Nelson's achievements as a tactician. For my own part, I may say with gratitude that but for Mr. Corbett's valuable work I could not have completed this article.

The most renowned of Nelson's achievements was that performed in his final battle and victory. Strange as it may seem, that celebrated performance has been the subject of much controversy, and, brilliant as it was, the tactics adopted in it have been freely, and indeed unfavourably, criticised. There is still much difference of opinion as to the preliminary movements, and as to the exact method by which Nelson's attack was made. It has been often asserted that the method really followed was not that which Nelson had expressly declared his intention of adopting. The question raised concerning this is a difficult one, and, until the appearance of Mr. Julian Corbett's recent work and the interesting volume on Trafalgar lately published by Mr. H. Newbolt, had not been fully discussed. The late Vice-Admiral P. H. Colomb contributed to the 'United Service Magazine' of September 1899 a very striking article on the subject of Nelson's tactics in his last battle, and those who propose to study the case should certainly peruse what he wrote.

The criticism of Nelson's procedure at Trafalgar in its strongest form may be summarised as follows. It is affirmed that he drew

[1] *Nelson and the Neapolitan Jacobins.*
[2] *Fighting Instructions*, 1530, 1816.

up and communicated to the officers under his orders a certain plan of attack; that just before the battle he changed his plan without warning; that he hurried on his attack unnecessarily; that he exposed his fleet to excessive peril; and, because of all this, that the British loss was much heavier and much less evenly distributed among the ships of the fleet than it need have been. The most formidable arraignment of the mode of Nelson's last attack is, undoubtedly, to be found in the paper published by Sir Charles Ekins in his book on 'Naval Battles,' and vouched for by him as the work of an eyewitness—almost certainly, as Mr. Julian Corbett holds, an officer on board the *Conqueror* in the battle. It is a remarkable document. Being critical rather than instructive, it is not to be classed with the essay of Clerk of Eldin; but it is one of the most important contributions to the investigation of tactical questions ever published in the English tongue. On it are based nearly, or quite, all the unfavourable views expressed concerning the British tactics at Trafalgar. As it contains a respectfully stated, but still sharp, criticism of Nelson's action, it will not be thought presumptuous if we criticise it in its turn.

Notwithstanding the fact that the author of the paper actually took part in the battle, and that he was gifted with no mean tactical insight, it is permissible to say that his remarks have an academic tinge. In fact, they are very much of the kind that a clever professor of tactics, who had not felt the responsibilities inseparable from the command of a fleet, would put before a class of students. Between a professor of tactics, however clever, and a commanding genius like Nelson the difference is great indeed. The writer of the paper in question perhaps expressed the more general opinion of his day. He has certainly suggested opinions to later generations of naval officers. The captains who shared in Nelson's last great victory did not agree among themselves as to the mode in which the attack was introduced. It was believed by some of them, and, thanks largely to the *Conqueror* officer's paper, it is generally believed now, that, whereas Nelson had announced his intention of advancing to the attack in lines-abreast or lines-of-bearing, he really did so in lines-ahead. Following up the path of investigation to which, in his article above mentioned, Admiral Colomb had already pointed, we can, I think, arrive only at the conclusion that the announced intention was adhered to.

Before the reasons for this conclusion are given it will be convenient to deal with the suggestions, or allegations, that Nelson exposed his fleet at Trafalgar to unduly heavy loss, putting it in the power of the enemy—to use the words of the *Conqueror's* officer—to ' have annihilated the ships one after another in detail ' ; and that ' the brunt of the action would have been more equally felt ' had a different mode of advance from that actually chosen been adopted. Now, Trafalgar was a battle in which an inferior fleet of twenty-six ships gained a victory over a superior fleet of thirty-three. The victory was so decisive that more than half of the enemy's capital ships were captured or destroyed on the spot, and the remainder were so battered that some fell an easy prey to the victor's side soon after the battle, the rest having limped painfully to the shelter of a fortified port near at hand. To gain such a victory over a superior force of seamen justly celebrated for their spirit and gallantry very hard fighting was necessary. The only actions of the Napoleonic period that can be compared with it are those of Camperdown, the Nile, and Copenhagen. The proportionate loss at Trafalgar was the least in all the four battles.[1] The allegation that, had Nelson followed a different method at Trafalgar, the ' brunt of the action would have been more equally felt ' can be disposed of easily. In nearly all sea-fights, whether Nelsonic in character or not, half of the loss of the victors has fallen on considerably less than half the fleet. That this has been the rule, whatever tactical method may have been adopted, will appear from the following statement. In Rodney's victory (April 12, 1782) half the loss fell upon nine ships out of thirty-six, or one-fourth ; at ' The First of June ' it fell upon five ships out of twenty-five, or one-fifth ; at St. Vincent it fell upon three ships out of fifteen, also one-fifth ; at Trafalgar half the loss fell on five ships out of twenty-seven, or very little less than an exact fifth. It has, therefore, been conclusively shown that, faulty or not faulty, long-announced or hastily adopted, the plan on which the battle of Trafalgar was fought did not occasion excessive loss to the victors or confine the loss, such as it was, to an unduly small portion of their fleet. As bearing on this question of the relative severity of the British loss at Trafalgar, it may be remarked that in that battle there were several British ships which had been in other great sea-fights. Their losses in these latter were in nearly every

---

[1] Camperdown .	.	.	. · 825 loss out of	8,221 : 10	per cent.
The Nile .	.	.	. 896 ,,	,, 7,401 : 12·1	,,
Copenhagen .	.	.	. 941 ,,	,, 6,892 : 13·75	,,
Trafalgar	.	.	. *1,690* ,,	,, *17,256 : 9·73*	,,

case heavier than their Trafalgar losses.[1] Authoritative and un-disputed figures show how baseless are the suggestions that Nelson's tactical procedure at Trafalgar caused his fleet to suffer needlessly heavy loss.

It is now necessary to investigate the statement that Nelson, hastily and without warning, changed his plan for fighting the battle. This investigation is much more difficult than that into the losses of the British fleet, because, whilst the latter can be settled by arithmetic, the former must proceed largely upon con-jecture. How desirable it is to make the investigation of the statement mentioned will be manifest when we reflect on the curious fact that the very completeness of Nelson's success at Trafalgar checked, or, indeed, virtually destroyed, the study of tactics in the British Navy for more than three-quarters of a century. His action was so misunderstood, or, at any rate, so variously represented, that it generally passed for gospel in our Service that Nelson's method consisted merely in rushing at his enemy as soon as he saw him. Against this conception his biographers, one after another, have protested in vain.

At the outset of this investigation it will be well to call to mind two or three things, simple enough, but not always remembered. One of these is that advancing to the attack and the attack itself are not the same operations. Another is, that, in the order of sailing in two or more columns, if the ships were 'by the wind' or close-hauled—the column-leaders were not abeam of each other, but bore from one another in the direction of the wind. Also, it may be mentioned that by simple alterations of course a line-abreast may be converted into a line-of-bearing and a line-

Ship	Action	Killed	Wounded	Total	Trafalgar		
					Killed	Wounded	Total
Ajax . . .	Rodney's (Ap. 12, 1782)	9	10	19	2	9	11
Agamemnon. .	„	15	22	37	2	8	10
Conqueror . .	„	7	22	29	3	9	12
Defence . .	1st June	17	36	53	7	29	36
Bellerophon. .	The Nile	49	148	197	27	123	150
Swiftsure . .	„	7	22	29	9	8	17
Defiance . .	Copenhagen	24	21	45	17	53	70
Polyphemus. .	„	6	25	31	2	4	6

In only one case was the Trafalgar total loss greater than the total loss of the same ship in an earlier fight ; and in this case (the *Defiance*) the number of killed at Trafalgar was only about two-thirds of the number killed in the other action.

of-bearing into a line-ahead, and that the reverse can be effected by the same operation. Again, adherence to a plan which presupposes the enemy's fleet to be in a particular formation after he is found to be in another is not to be expected of a consummate tactician. This remark is introduced here with full knowledge of the probability that it will be quoted as an admission that Nelson did change his plan without warning. No admission of the kind is intended. 'In all cases of anticipated battle,' says Mahan, 'Nelson was careful to put his subordinates in possession both of his general plans and, as far as possible, of the underlying ideas.' The same biographer tells us, what is well worth remember-

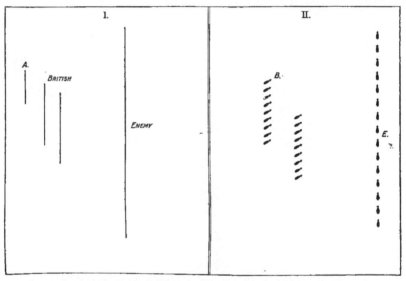

DIAGRAM EXPLAINING NELSON'S MEMORANDUM OF OCTOBER 9, 1805.
(This is generally attached to copies of the Memorandum.)

A. was the Advance Squadron to be distributed amongst the two British Divisions.
B. The way in which the British ships would have been placed in their Divisions if in exact station. The ships are heading so as to reach the points of attack in the enemy's line which is moving.
E. The same as regards the enemy.

ing, that 'No man was ever better served than Nelson by the inspiration of the moment; no man ever counted on it less.'

The plan announced in the celebrated memorandum of October 9, 1805, indicated, for the attack from to windward, that the British fleet, in what would be called on shore an echelon of two main divisions and an 'advance squadron,' would move

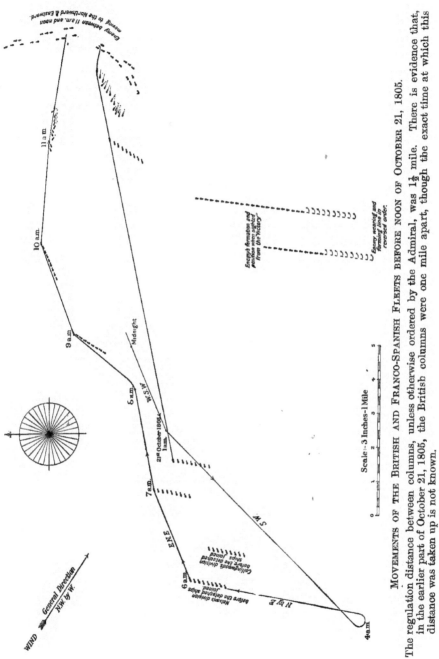

MOVEMENTS OF THE BRITISH AND FRANCO-SPANISH FLEETS BEFORE NOON OF OCTOBER 21, 1805.

The regulation distance between columns, unless otherwise ordered by the Admiral, was 1½ mile. There is evidence that, in the earlier part of October 21, 1805, the British columns were one mile apart, though the exact time at which this distance was taken up is not known.

against an enemy assumed to be in single line-ahead. The 'advance squadron,' it should be noted, was not to be ahead of the two main divisions, but in such a position that it could be moved to strengthen either. The name seems to have been due to the mode in which the ships composing the squadron were employed in, so to speak, 'feeling for' the enemy. On October 19 six ships were ordered 'to go ahead during the night'; and, besides the frigates, two more ships were so stationed as to keep up the communication between the six and the Commander-in-Chief's flagship. Thus eight ships in effect composed an 'advance squadron,' and did not join either of the main divisions at first.

When it was expected that the British fleet would comprise forty sail-of-the-line and the enemy's fleet forty-six, each British main division was to be made up of sixteen ships; and eight two-deckers added to either division would increase the strength of the latter to twenty-four ships. It is interesting to note that, omitting the *Africa*, which ship came up late, each British main division on the morning of October 21, 1805, had nine ships—a number which, by the addition of the eight already mentioned as distinct from the divisions, could have been increased to seventeen, thus, except for a fraction, exactly maintaining the original proportion as regards the hostile fleet, which was now found to be composed of thirty-three ships.

During the night of October 20–21 the Franco-Spanish fleet, which had been sailing in three divisions and a ' squadron of observation,' formed line and stood to the southward, heading a little to the eastward of south. The 'squadron of observation' was parallel to the main body and to windward (in this case to the westward) of it, with the leading ships rather more advanced.

The British main divisions steered W.S.W. till 1 A.M. After that they steered S.W. till 4 A.M. There are great difficulties about the time, as the notation of it [1] differed considerably in different ships; but the above hours are taken from the *Victory's* log. At 4 A.M. the British fleet, or rather its main divisions, wore and stood N. by E. As the wind was about N.W. by W., the ships were close-hauled, and the leader of the 'lee-line,' *i.e.* Collingwood's flagship, was when in station two points abaft the *Victory's* beam

---

[1] Except the chronometers, which were instruments of navigation so precious as always to be kept under lock and key, there were no clocks in the Navy till some years after I joined it. Time on board ship was kept by half-hour sand-glasses.

as soon as the ' order of sailing ' in two columns—which was to be the order of battle—had been formed.

About 6 A.M. the enemy's fleet was sighted from the *Victory*, and observed to bear from her E. by S. and be distant from her ten or twelve miles. The distance is corroborated by observed bearings from Collingwood's flagship.[1] Viewed from the British ships, placed as they were relatively to it, the enemy's fleet must have appeared as a long single line-ahead, perhaps not very exactly formed. As soon as the hostile force was clearly made out, the British divisions bore up and stood to the eastward, steering by the *Victory's* compass E.N.E. The position and formation of the British main divisions were by this made exactly those in which they are shown in the diagram usually attached to the celebrated memorandum of October 9, 1805. The enemy must have appeared to the British, who were ten or twelve miles to windward of him, and on his beam, as if he were formed in line-ahead. He therefore was also in the position and formation assigned to him in that diagram.

At a time which, because of the variety in the notations of it, it is difficult to fix exactly, but somewhere between 7 and 8 A.M., the enemy's ships wore together and endeavoured to form a line to the northward, which, owing to the direction of the wind, must have been about N. by E. and S. by W., or N.N.E. and S.S.W. The operation—not merely of wearing, but of both wearing and reforming the line, such as it was—took more than an hour to complete. The wind was light; there was a westerly swell; the ships were under easy sail; consequently there must have been a good deal of leeway, and the hostile or ' combined ' fleet headed in the direction of Cadiz, towards which, we are expressly told by a high French authority—Chevalier—it advanced.

Nelson had to direct the course of his fleet so that its divisions, when about to make the actual attack, would be just opposite the points to which the respective hostile ships had advanced in the meantime. In a light wind varying in force a direct course to those points could not be settled once for all; but that first chosen was very nearly right, and an alteration of a point, viz. to E. by N., was for a considerable time all that was necessary. Collingwood later

---

[1] It would necessitate the use of some technicalities to explain it fully; but it may be said that the bearings of the extremes of the enemy's line observed from his flagship prove that Collingwood was in the station that he ought to have occupied when the British fleet was in the Order of Sailing and close to the wind.

made a signal to his division to alter course one point to port, which brought them back to the earlier course, which by the *Victory's* compass had been E.N.E. The eight ships of what has been referred to as the 'advance squadron' were distributed between the two main British divisions, six being assigned to Collingwood's and two to Nelson's. They did not all join their divisions at the same time, some—probably owing to the distance at which they had been employed from the rest of the fleet and the feebleness of the breeze—not till several hours after the combined fleet had been sighted.

Collingwood preserved in his division a line-of-bearing apparently until the very moment when the individual ships pushed on to make the actual attack. The enemy's fleet is usually represented as forming a curve. It would probably be more correct to call it a very obtuse re-entering angle. This must have been largely due to Gravina's 'squadron of observation' keeping away in succession, to get into the wake of the rest of the line, which was forming towards the north. About the centre of the combined fleet there was a gap of a mile. Ahead and astern of this the ships were not all in each other's wake. Many were to leeward of their stations, thus giving the enemy's formation the appearance of a double line, or rather of a string of groups of ships. It is important to remember this, because no possible mode of attack—the enemy's fleet being formed as it was—could have prevented some British ships from being 'doubled on' when they cut into the enemy's force. On 'The First of June,' notwithstanding that the advance to the attack was intended to be in line-abreast, several British ships were 'doubled on,' and even 'trebled on,' as will be seen in the experiences on that day of the *Brunswick*, *Marlborough*, *Royal Sovereign*, and *Queen Charlotte* herself.

Owing to the shape of the hostile 'line' at Trafalgar and the formation in which he kept his division, Collingwood brought his ships, up till the very moment when each proceeded to deliver her attack, in the formation laid down in the oft-quoted memorandum. By the terms of that document Nelson had specifically assigned to his own division the work of seeing that the movements of Collingwood's division should be interrupted as little as possible. It would, of course, have been beyond his power to do this if the position of his own division in the echelon formation prescribed in the memorandum had been rigorously adhered to after Collingwood was getting near his objective point. In execution, therefore, of the service allotted to his division Nelson made a feint at the enemy's van. This necessitated an alteration of course to port, so that his ships came into a 'line-of-bearing' so very oblique that it may well have been loosely called a 'line-ahead.' Sir Charles Ekins says that the two British lines ' *afterwards* fell into line-ahead, the ships in the wake of each other,' and that this was in obedience to signal. Collingwood's line certainly did not fall into line-ahead. At the most it was a rather oblique line-of-bearing almost parallel to that part of the enemy's fleet which he was about to attack. In Nelson's line there was more than one alteration of course, as the *Victory's* log expressly states that she kept standing for the enemy's van, which we learn from the French accounts was moving about N. by E. or N.N.E. In the light wind prevailing the alterations of course must have rendered it, towards the end of the forenoon, impossible to keep exact station, even if the *Victory* were to shorten sail, which we know she did not. As Admiral Colomb pointed out, ' Several later signals are recorded which were proper to make in lines-of-bearing, but not in lines-ahead.' It is difficult to import into this fact any other meaning but that of intention to preserve, however obliquely, the line-of-bearing which undoubtedly had been formed by the act of bearing-up as soon as the enemy's fleet had been distinguished.

When Collingwood had moved near enough to the enemy to let his ships deliver their attacks it became unnecessary for Nelson's division to provide against the other's being interrupted. Accordingly, he headed for the point at which he meant to cut into the enemy's fleet. Now came the moment, as regards his division, for doing what Collingwood's had already begun to do, viz. engage in a 'pell-mell battle,' [1] which surely may be interpreted as meaning a battle in which rigorous station-keeping was no longer expected, and in which ' no captain could do very wrong if he placed his ship alongside that of the enemy.'

In several diagrams of the battle as supposed to have been fought the two British divisions just before the moment of impact are represented as converging towards each other. The Spanish diagram, lately reproduced by Mr. Newbolt, shows this, as well as the English diagrams. We may take it, therefore, that there was towards the end of the forenoon a convergence of the two columns, and that this was due to Nelson's return from his feint at the hostile van to the line from which he intended to let go his

---

[1] Nelson's own expression.

ships to deliver the actual attack. Collingwood's small alteration of course of one point to port slightly, but only slightly, accentuated this convergence.

Enough has been said here of Nelson's tactics at Trafalgar. To discuss them fully would require a whole treatise.

I can only express the hope that in the Navy the subject will receive fuller consideration hereafter. Nelson's last victory was gained, be it remembered, in one afternoon, over a fleet more than 20 per cent. its superior in numbers, and was so decisive that more than half of the hostile ships were taken. This was the crowning effort of seven years spent in virtually independent command in time of war—seven years, too, illustrated by more than one great victory.

The more closely we look into Nelson's tactical achievements, the more effective and brilliant do they appear. It is the same with his character and disposition. The more exact researches and investigations of recent times have removed from his name the obloquy which it pleased some to cast upon it. We can see now that his ' childlike, delighted vanity '—to use the phrase of his greatest biographer—was but a thin incrustation on noble qualities. As in the material world valueless earthy substances surround a vein of precious metal, so through Nelson's moral nature there ran an opulent lode of character, unimpaired in its priceless worth by adjacent frailties which, in the majority of mankind, are present without any precious stuff beneath them. It is with minds prepared to see this that we should commemorate our great Admiral.

Veneration of Nelson's memory cannot be confined to particular objects or be limited by locality. His tomb is wider than the space covered by dome or column, and his real monument is more durable than any material construction. It is the unwritten and spiritual memorial of him, firmly fixed in the hearts of his fellow-countrymen.

Lightning Source UK Ltd.
Milton Keynes UK
UKHW040614090519
342383UK00002B/734/P

9 781473 321656